Meditative Tracing & Coloring
Flower Mandalas

Terri Clauss

Coloring Techniques, Tips, and Affirmations

COLORING CREDITS
@INSTAGRAM

FAITH D PARKS
@SUNSHOWERDESIGNS
- THE COURT OF CAMELLIA

ASHLIE ZEIDLER
@ASHZEIDLER
- DAISY & THE BERRIES

DIANA TAYLOR
@ALETHIAARTISTRY
- RAINBOW WREATH

TERRI CLAUSS
@LIGHTGIRLDESIGN
- FLORIDA WILD
- POPPY MAGIC
- DOTTY COLUMBINES
- CONEFLOWER ATTENDANTS
- TROPICAL PARADISE
- ORCHID HYDRANGEA BALL
- FLOWER GEOMETRY
- STARGAZER
- FRONDS & FRIENDS

CONTENTS

2. COLORING CREDITS

3. CONTENTS

4. INTRODUCTION

5. MATERIALS

AFFIRMATION
7. FLORIDA WILD

TECHNIQUE
9. POPPY MAGIC

Creativity is encouraged

AFFIRMATION
11. DAISY AND THE BERRIES

TECHNIQUE
13. CONEFLOWER ATTENDANTS

AFFIRMATION
15. DOTTY COLUMBINES

TECHNIQUE
17. THE COURT OF CAMELLIA

AFFIRMATION
19. TROPICAL PARADISE

TECHNIQUE
21. ORCHID HYDRANGEA BALL

AFFIRMATION
23. FLOWER GEOMETRY

TECHNIQUE
25. RAINBOW WREATH

AFFIRMATION
27. STARGAZER

TECHNIQUE
29. FRONDS & FRIENDS

CRAFT IDEAS & COMMUNITY

ART AS THERAPY

Some principles:
- Creativity is good for soul and synapses.
- Coloring is art.
- Tracing works as a mindfulness practice.
- You don't have to hang paintings in a gallery to enjoy artistic creativity.
- Enjoying an artistic creative practice transcends having drawing skills.
- It matters not in the slightest bit what others' art looks like.
- Un-plugging from our technological world and immersing yourself in color is a gateway to tranquility, gratitude , clarity, and joy.

You are invited to use your coloring time as a powerful tool for inner healing and insight, attracting good things to your life, shifting your perspective, sending goodwill to others, and even influencing the world.

How?
- Simply state that you dedicate this time and creation to (your intention)
- Dwell on the affirmation on the facing page or your own intention.
- Reinforce your desires by lightly penciling them in before coloring or by lighting a candle.
- Get on with your coloring, and smile, knowing that you have set something powerful into motion.

Each time you come back, flip through the pages you have already used. Notice what you have learned and how your skills have grown. Reaffirm the intentions that have not yet appeared and express gratitude for those that have.

Enjoy what you have created out of dull gray lines. Practice grace toward what you think is imperfect and consider directing that energy toward yourself and others.

MATERIALS
You have permission to mix mediums!

You will find that some work well together and some do not, but the joy is in the discovering.

- Get the best set of colored pencils you can afford. Prismacolor and Faber-Castell have student lines that are quite lovely. But don't judge! Crayola is perfectly fine.
- A fine black line marker or pen
- Colored markers:
- Water color brush pens (Try creatology at Target)
- Crayons (good for the larger spaces.)
- Chalk or oil pastels
- A white gel pen
- Colored gel pens
- Metallic pens and markers

Watercolor Paints, Watercolor Pencils & Paint Pens

If you wish to paint your line art, transfer the design to a heavier water color paper (for budget watercolor paper, look in the kids' art section.)

- Transfer it by hand with carbon paper (or just by scribbling on the back with a soft pencil.)
- Make a photocopy putting watercolor paper in the paper tray
- Photograph or scan your book and send the file to your home printer with watercolor paper in the paper tray.

Even though I feel flawed and inadequate sometimes, I am deserving of a beautiful, abundant, and safe life.

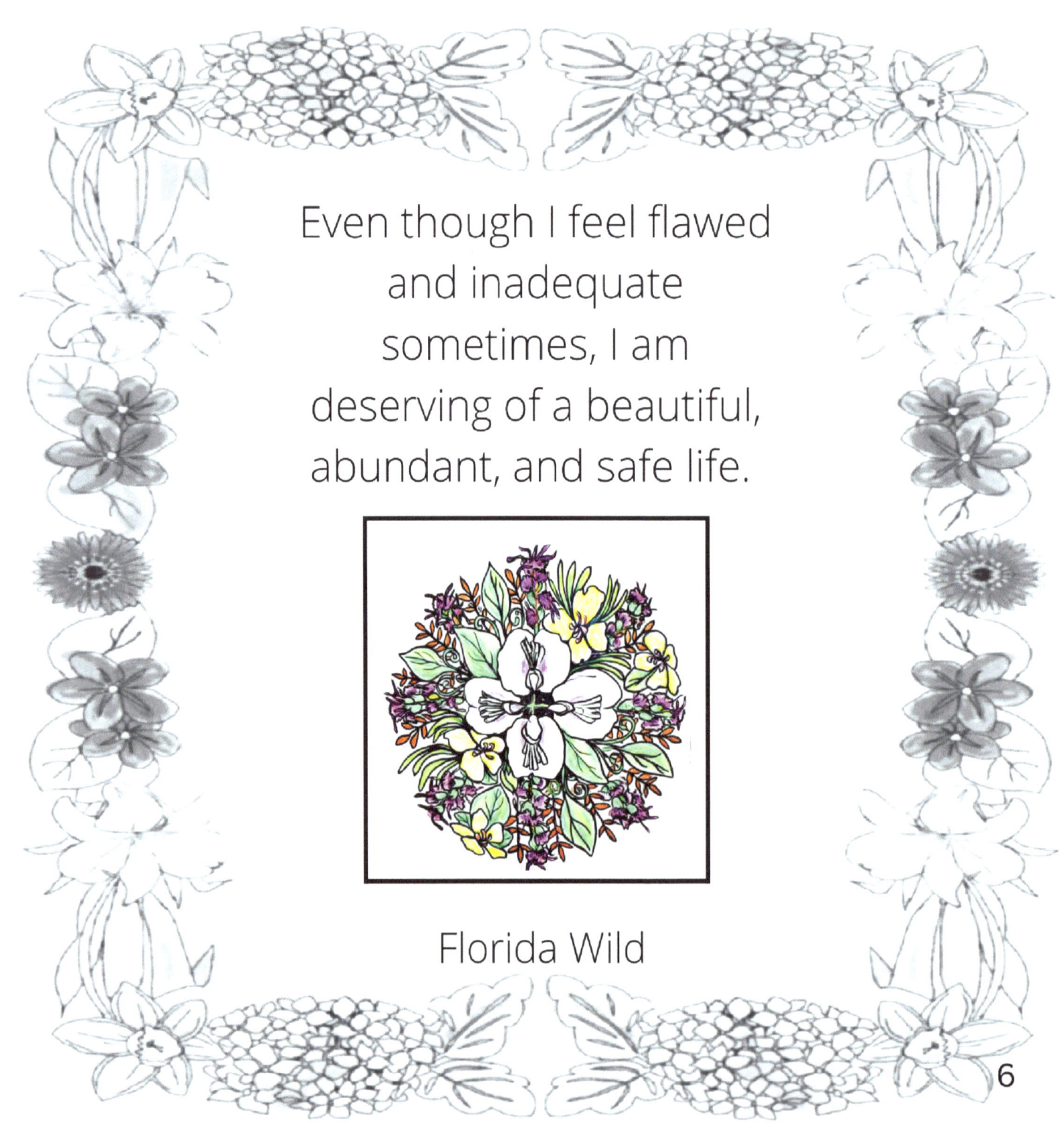

Florida Wild

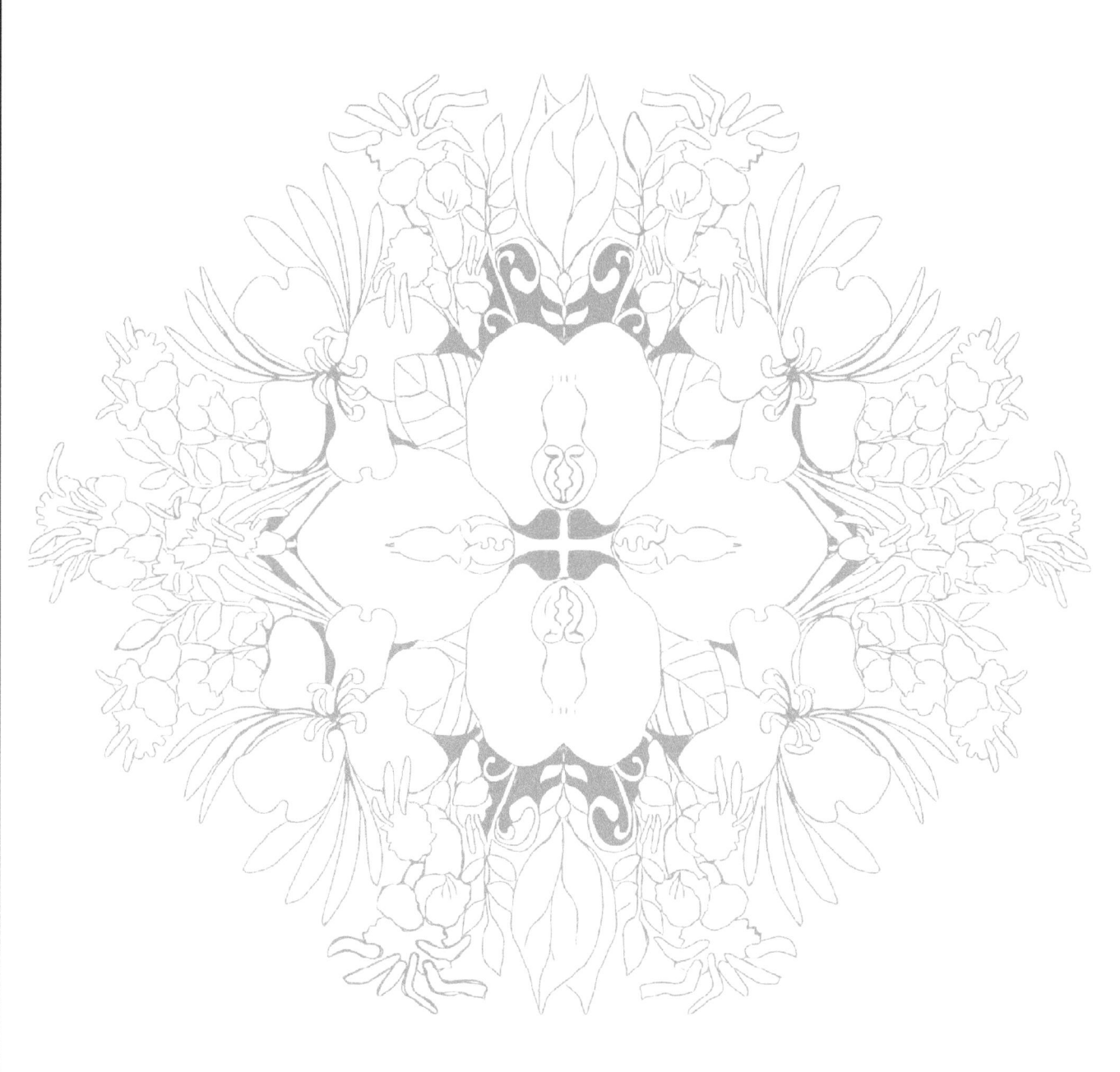

A technique to try

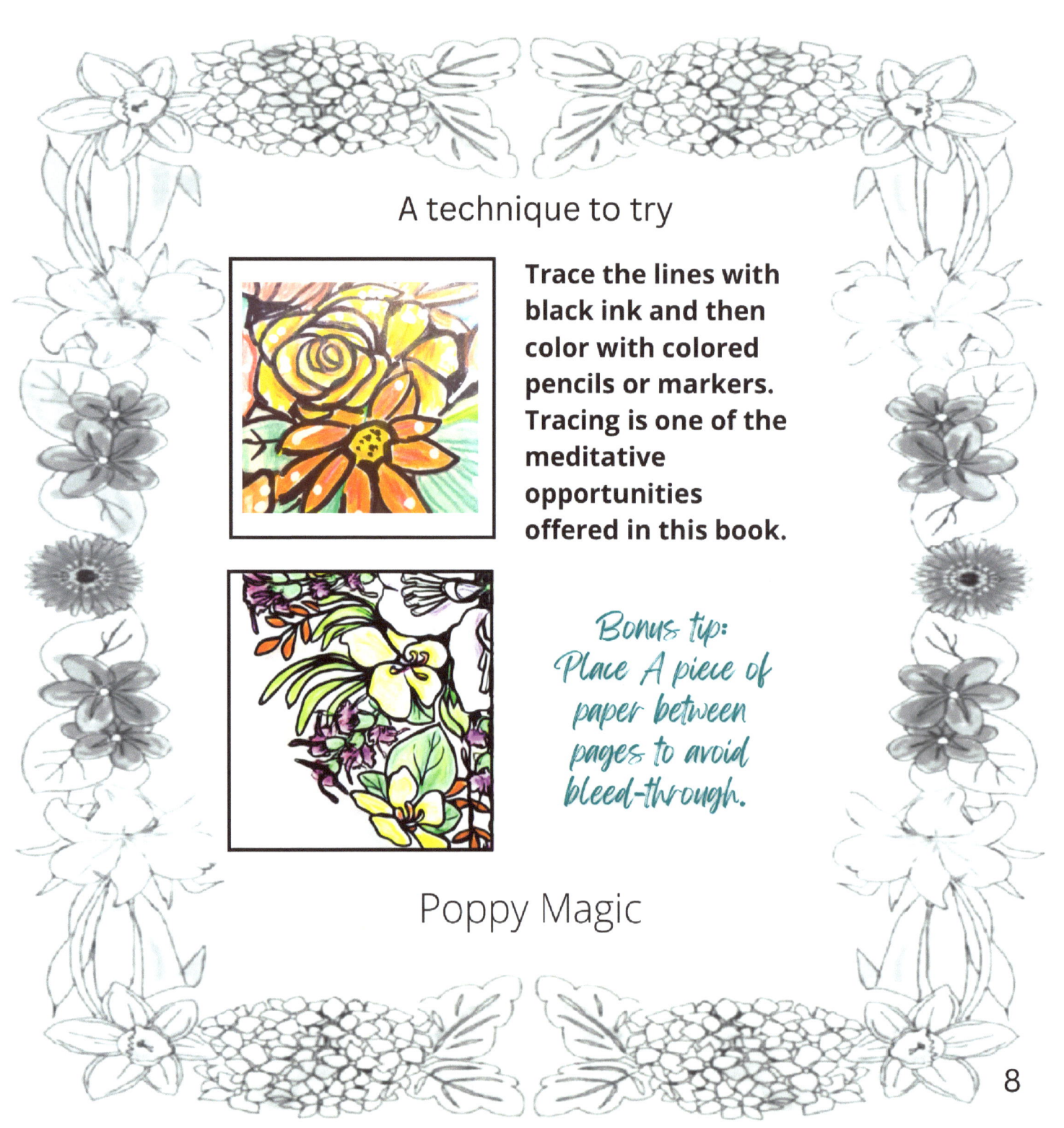

Trace the lines with black ink and then color with colored pencils or markers. Tracing is one of the meditative opportunities offered in this book.

Bonus tip: Place A piece of paper between pages to avoid bleed-through.

Poppy Magic

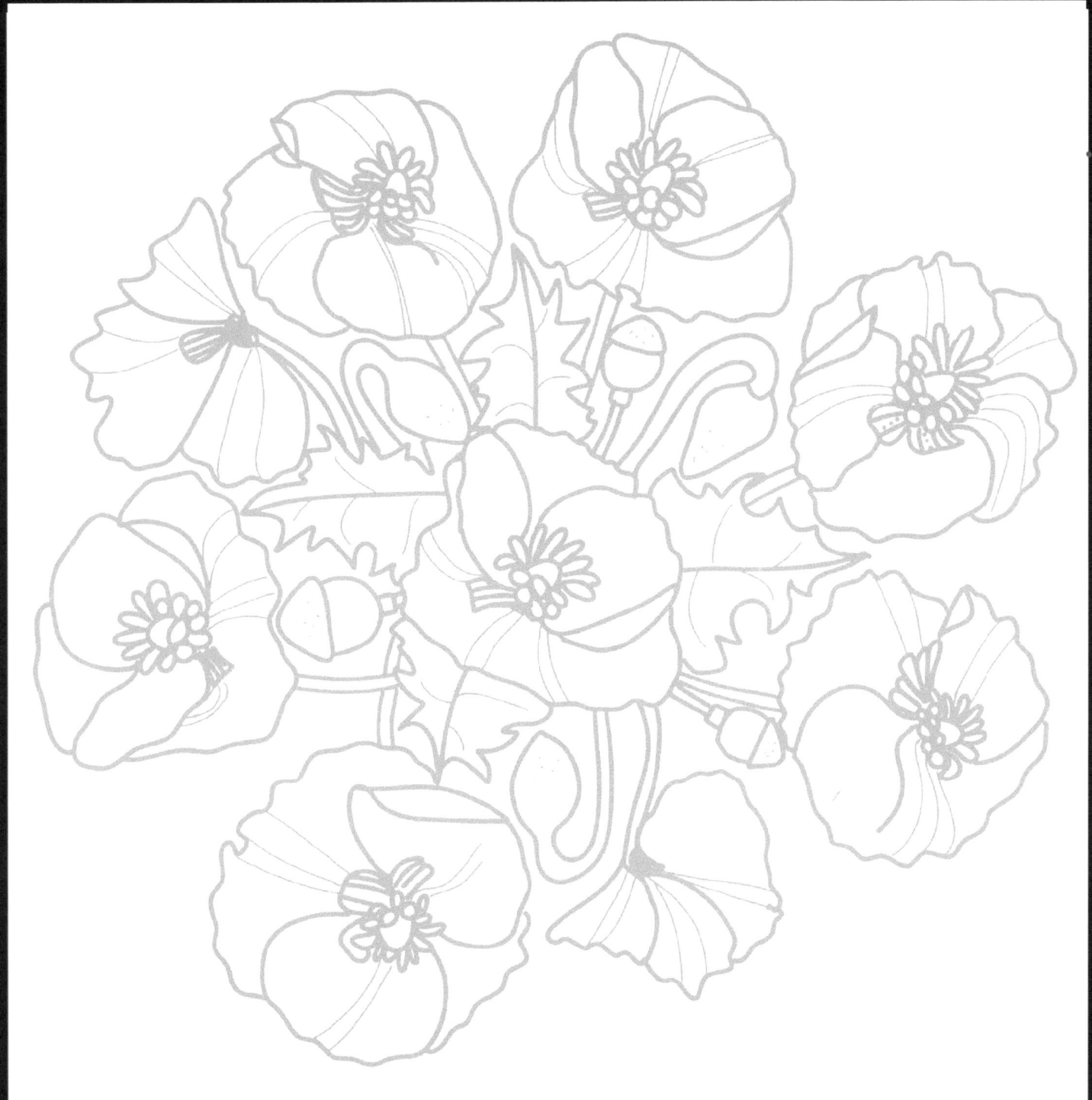

Ha! I can't even remember what my limiting beliefs are anymore.

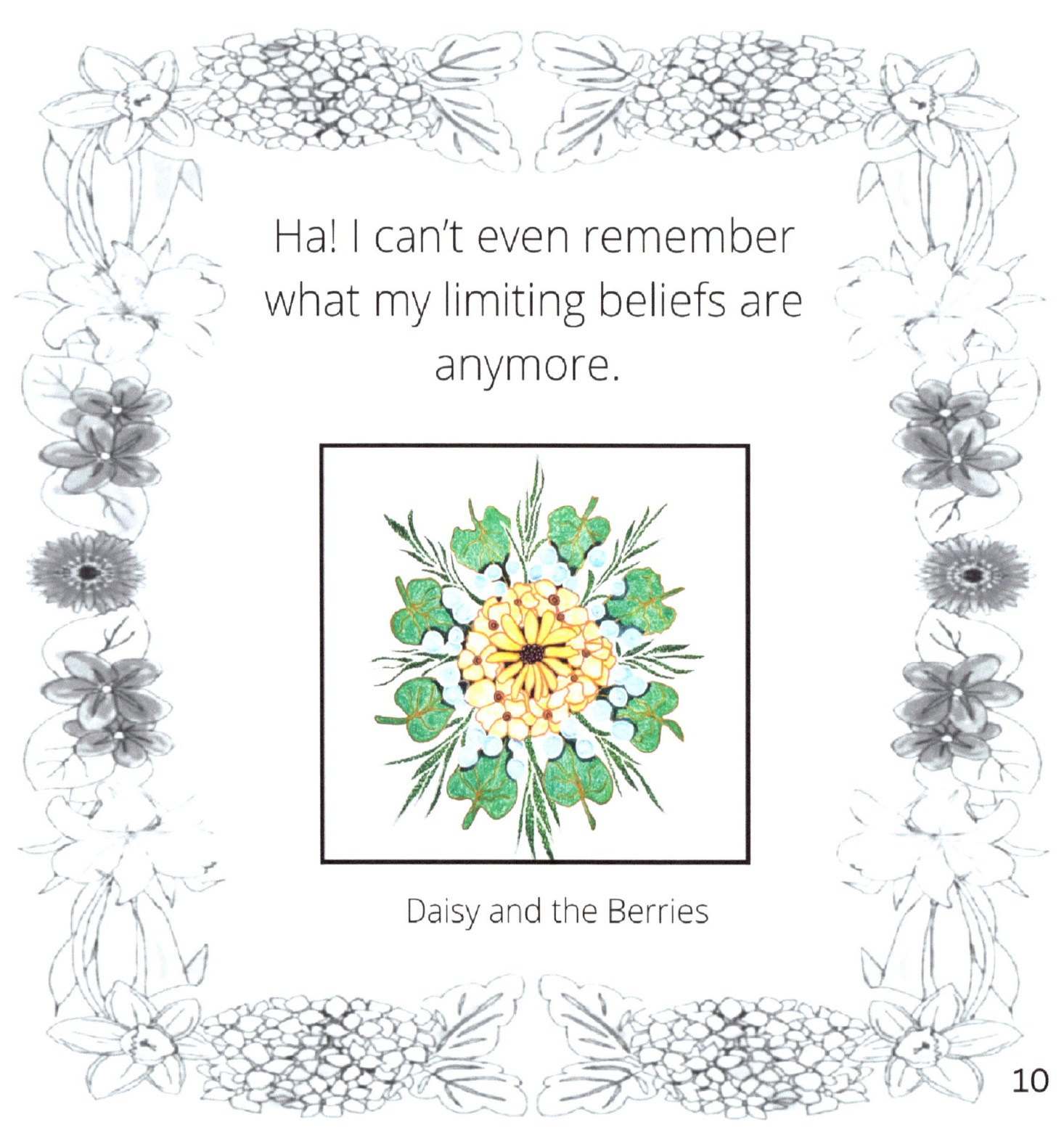

Daisy and the Berries

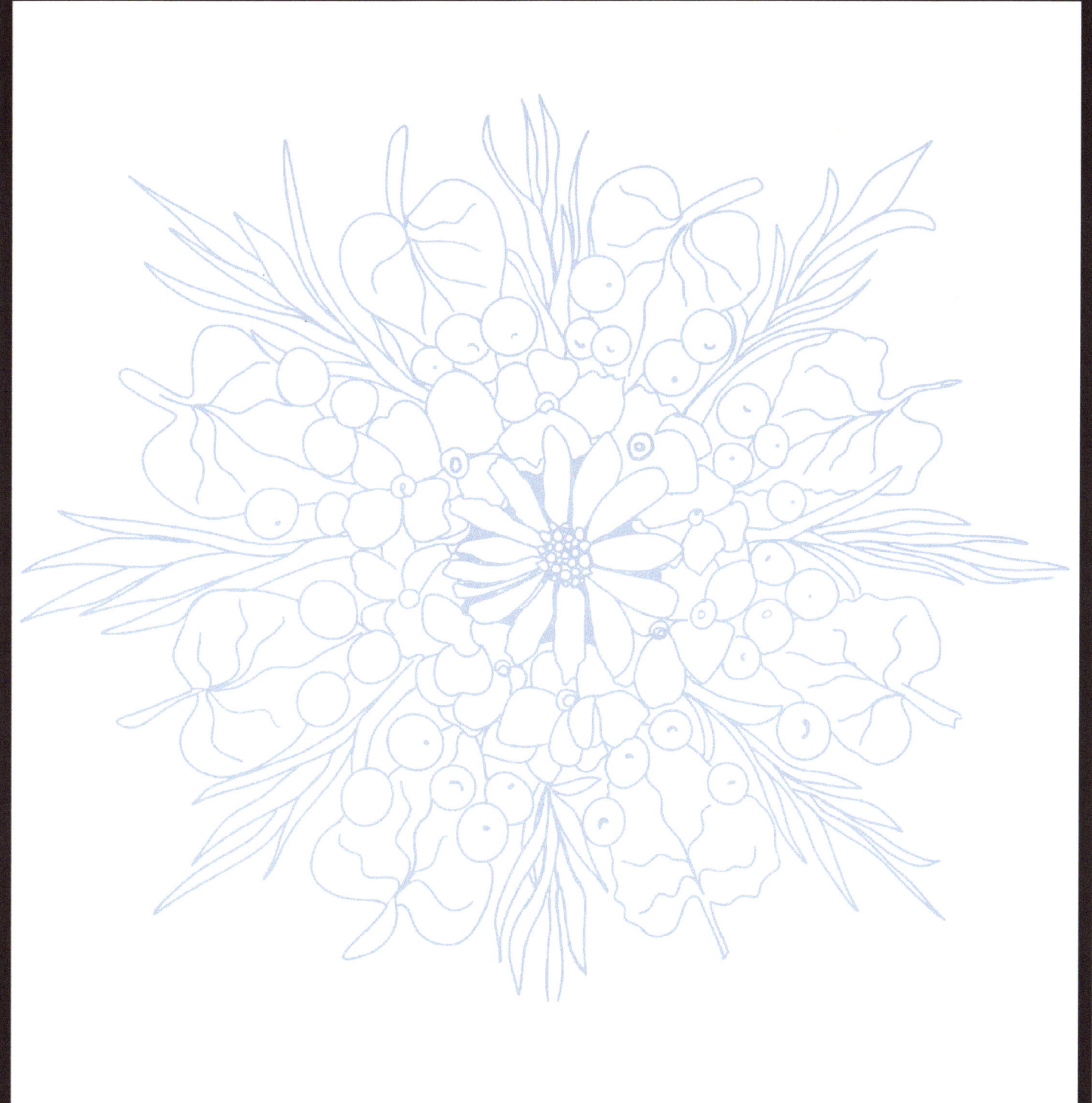

A technique to try

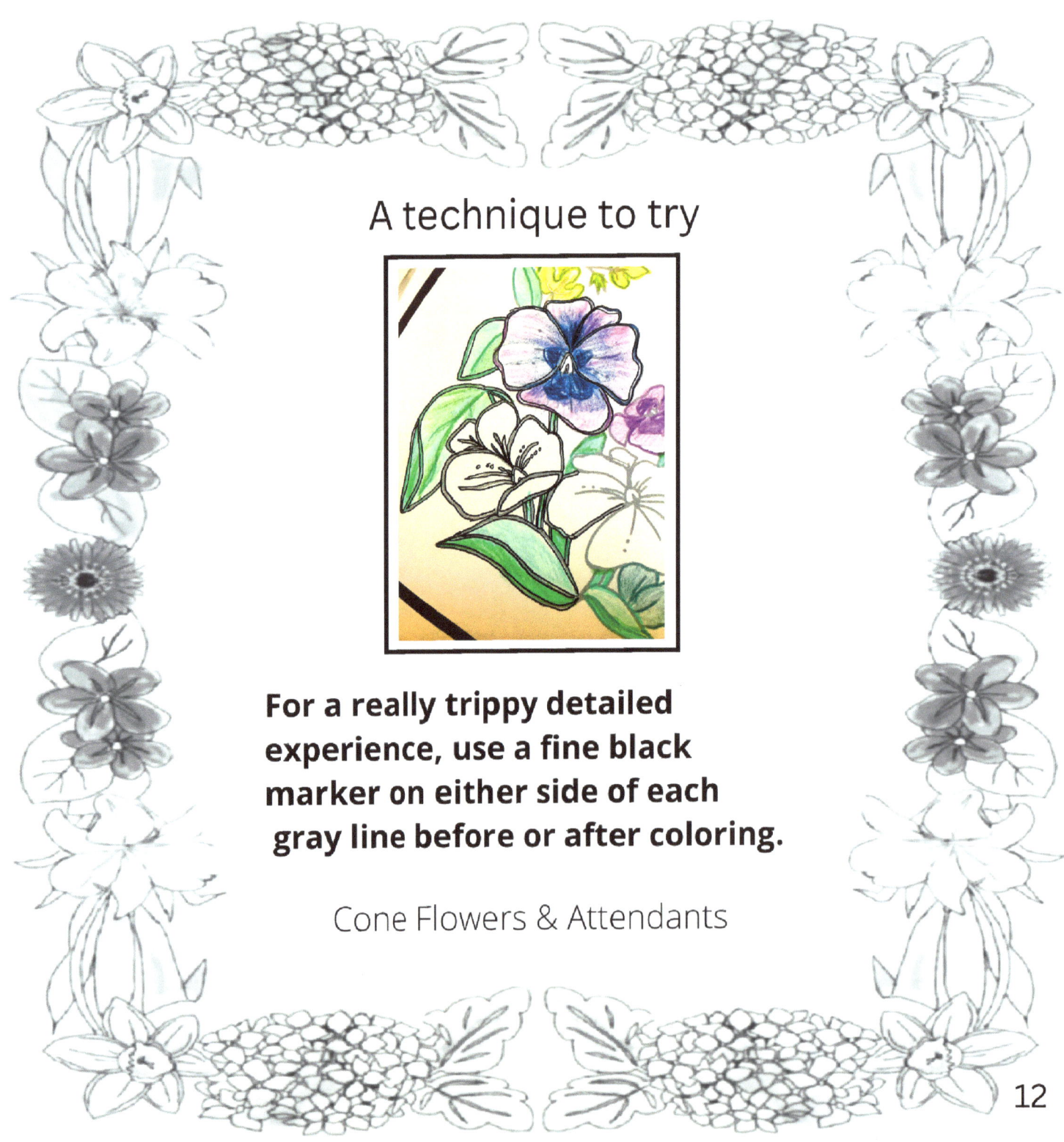

For a really trippy detailed experience, use a fine black marker on either side of each gray line before or after coloring.

Cone Flowers & Attendants

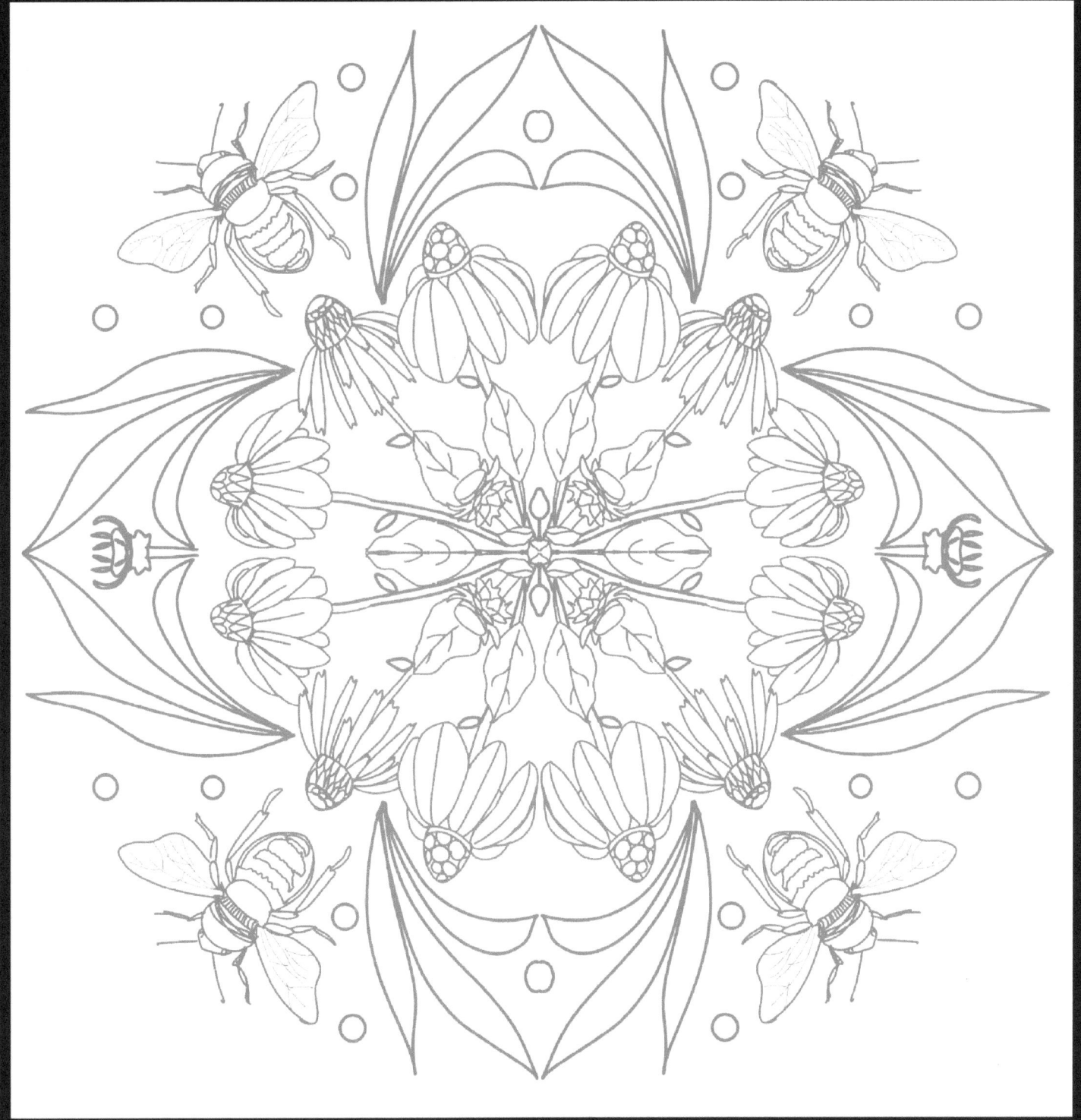

Wow! Why do I feel so confident and free?

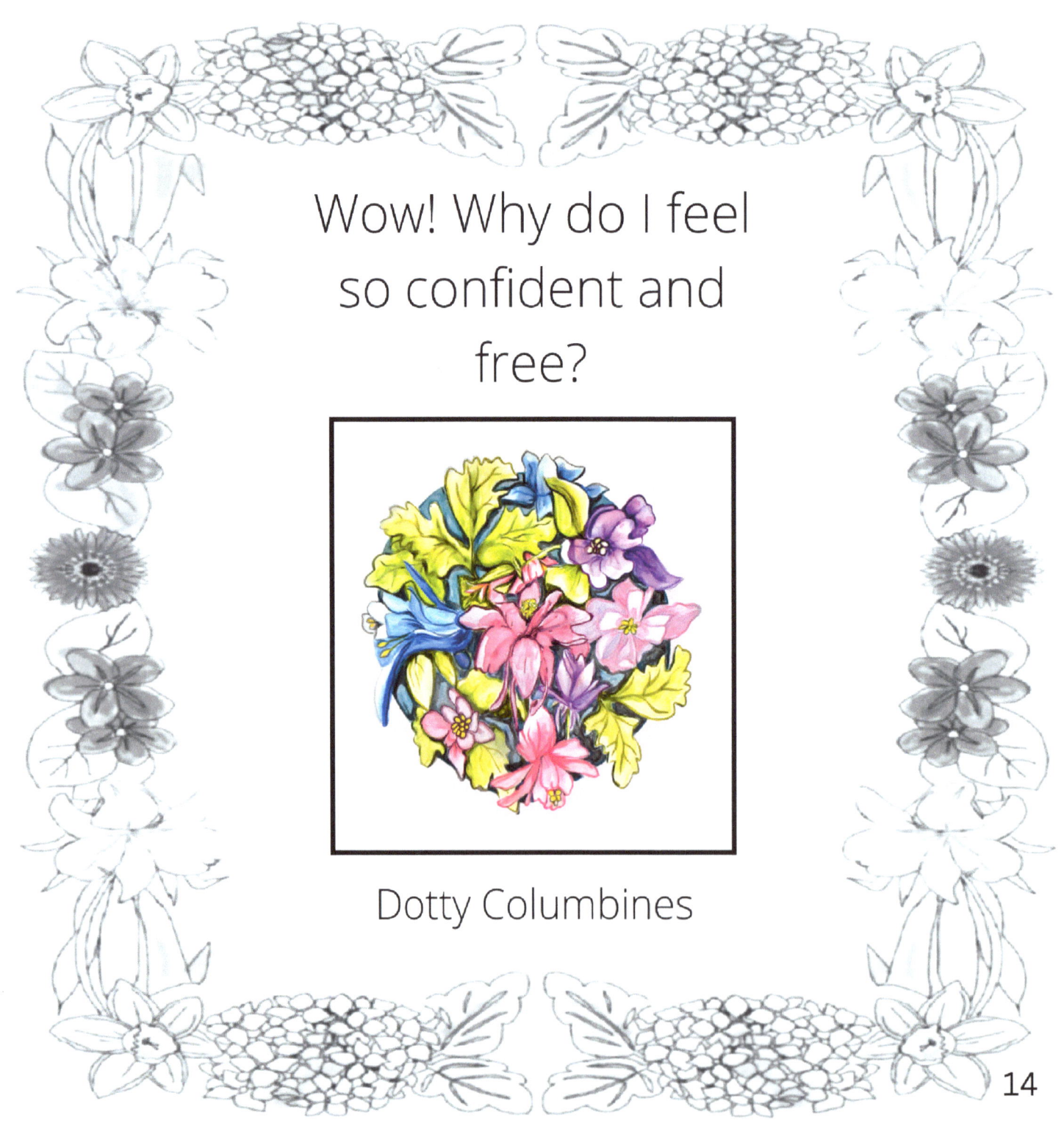

Dotty Columbines

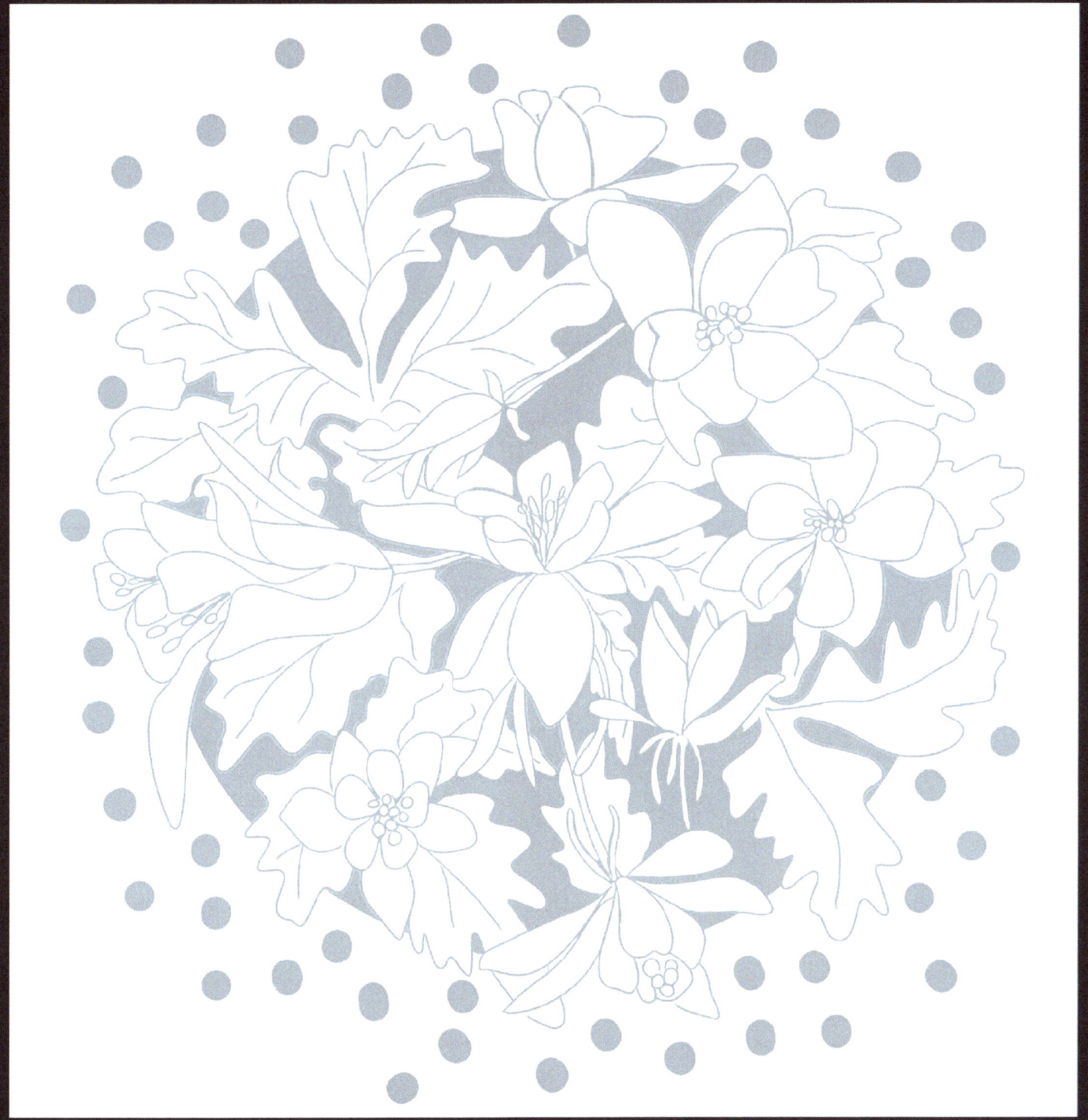

A technique to try

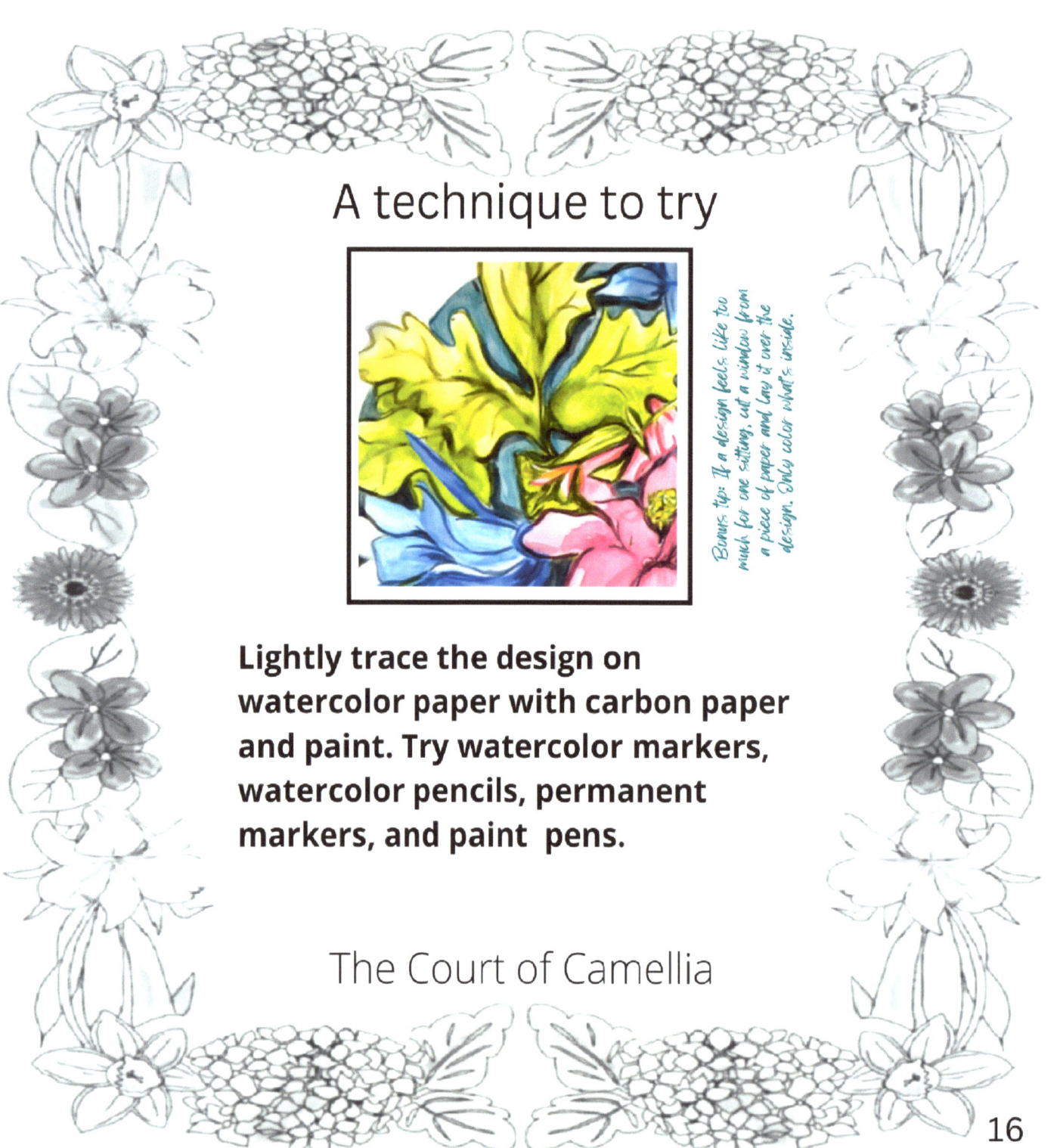

Bonus tip: If a design feels like too much for one sitting, cut a window from a piece of paper and lay it over the design. Only color what's inside.

Lightly trace the design on watercolor paper with carbon paper and paint. Try watercolor markers, watercolor pencils, permanent markers, and paint pens.

The Court of Camellia

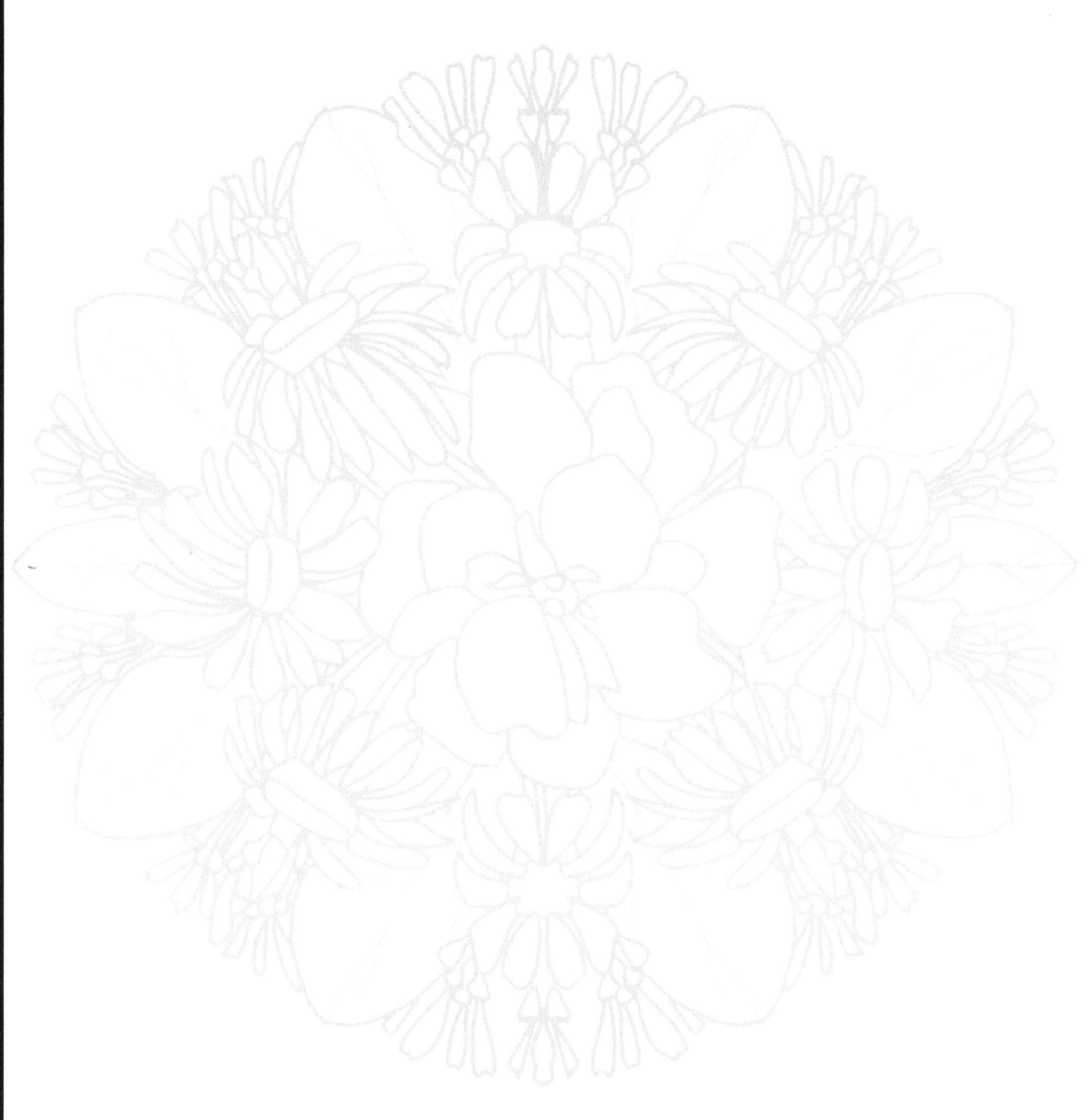

I'm becoming more
and more courageous
even in the face of
perilous times.

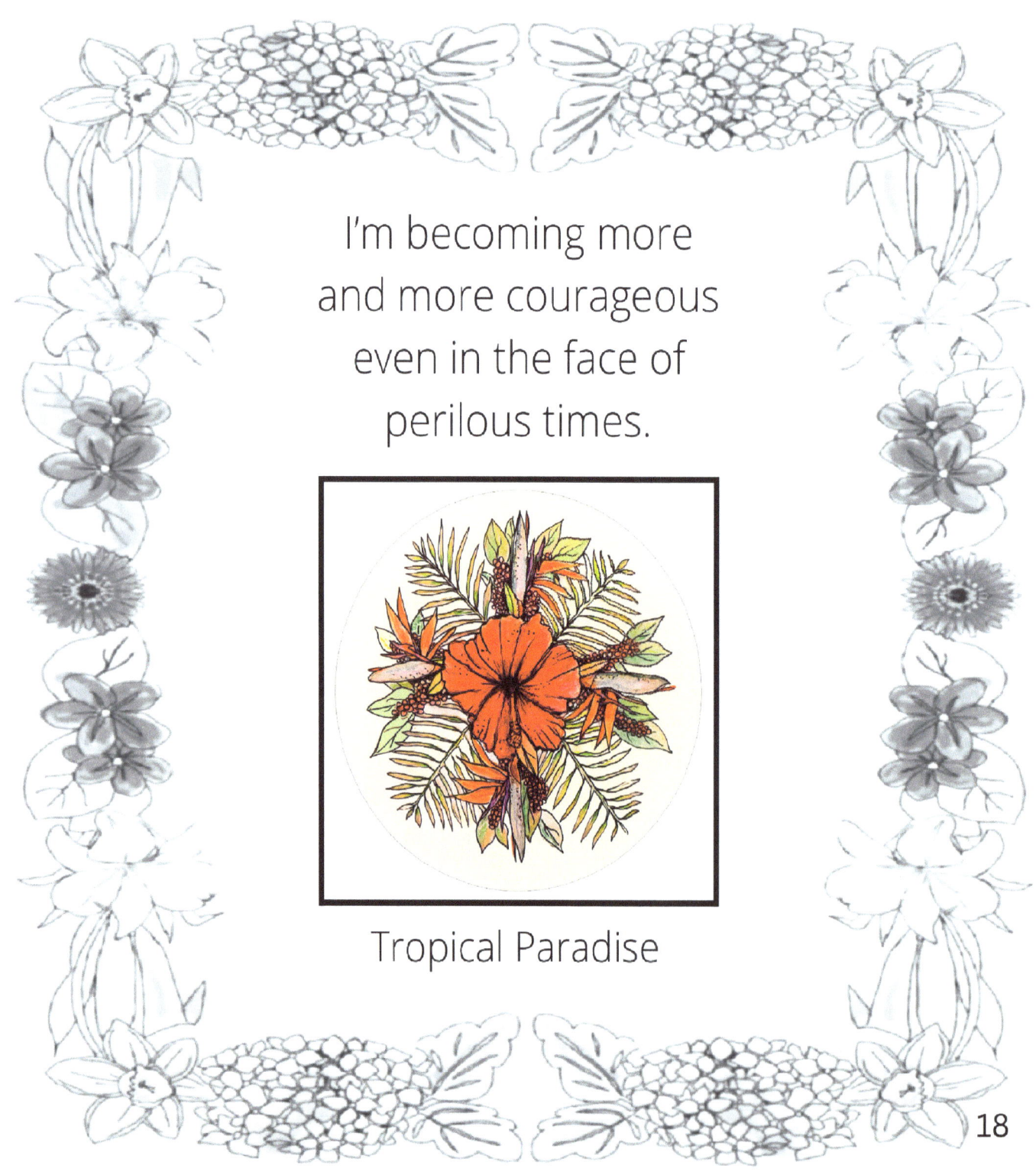

Tropical Paradise

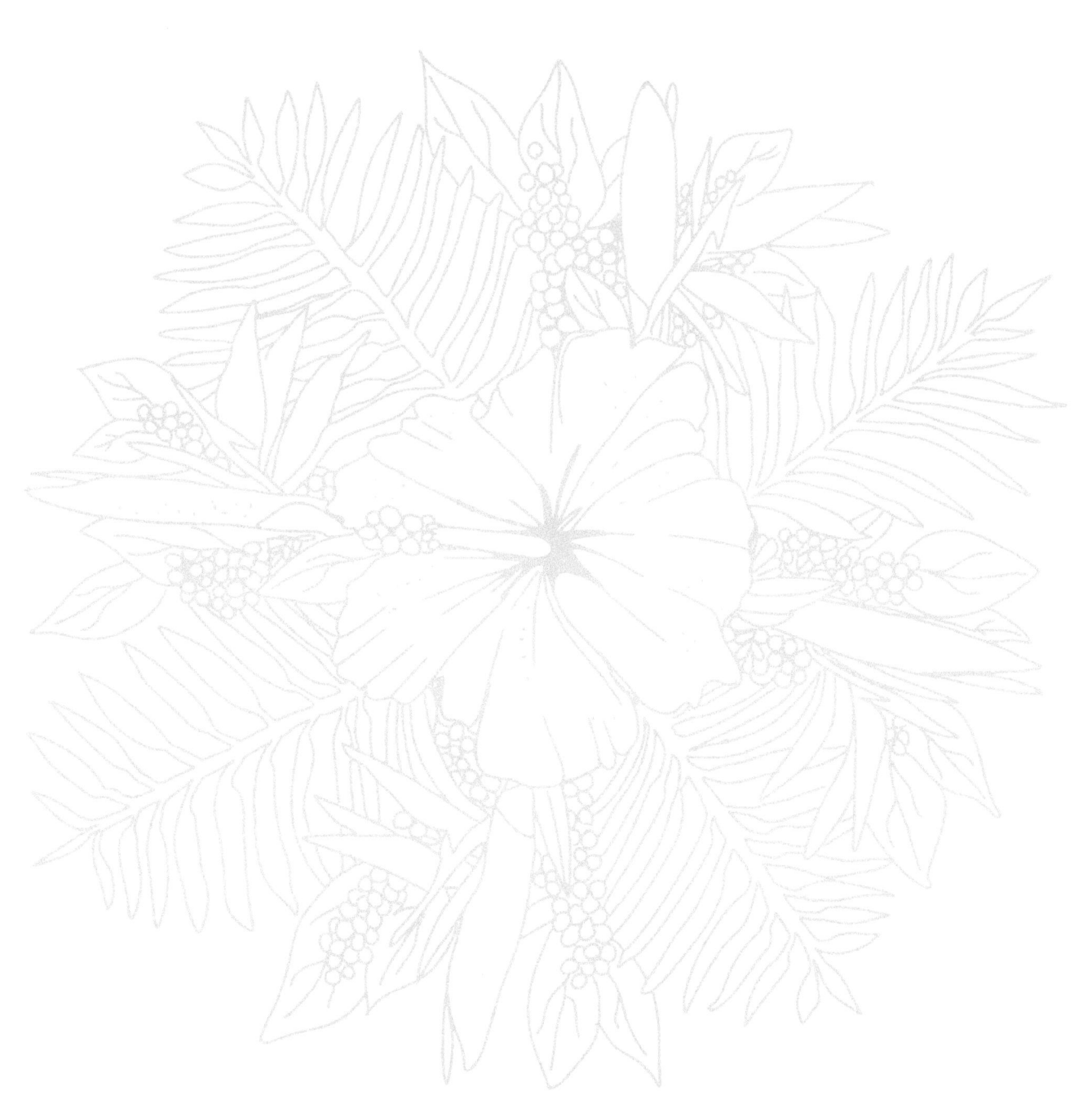

A technique to try

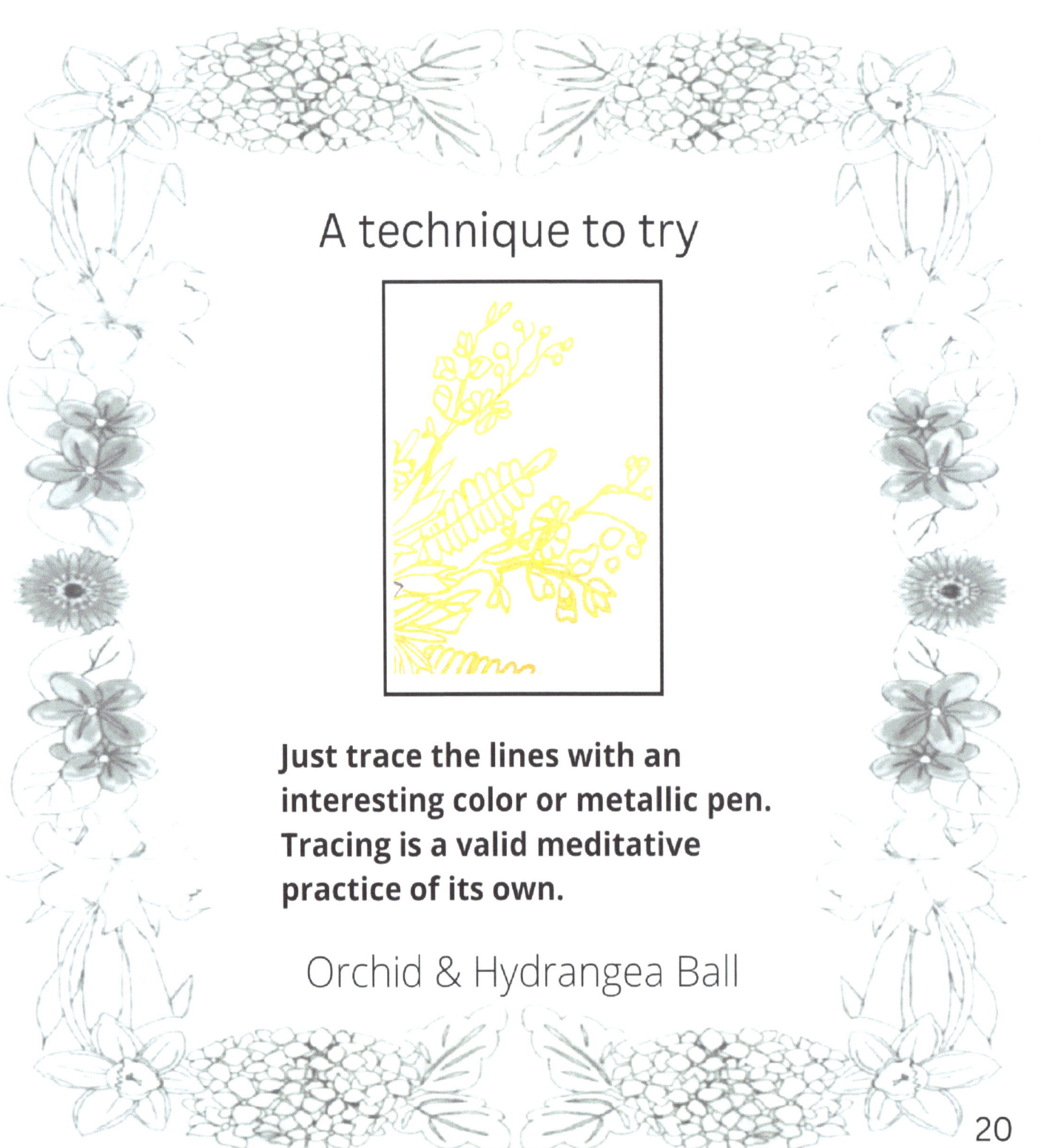

Just trace the lines with an interesting color or metallic pen. Tracing is a valid meditative practice of its own.

Orchid & Hydrangea Ball

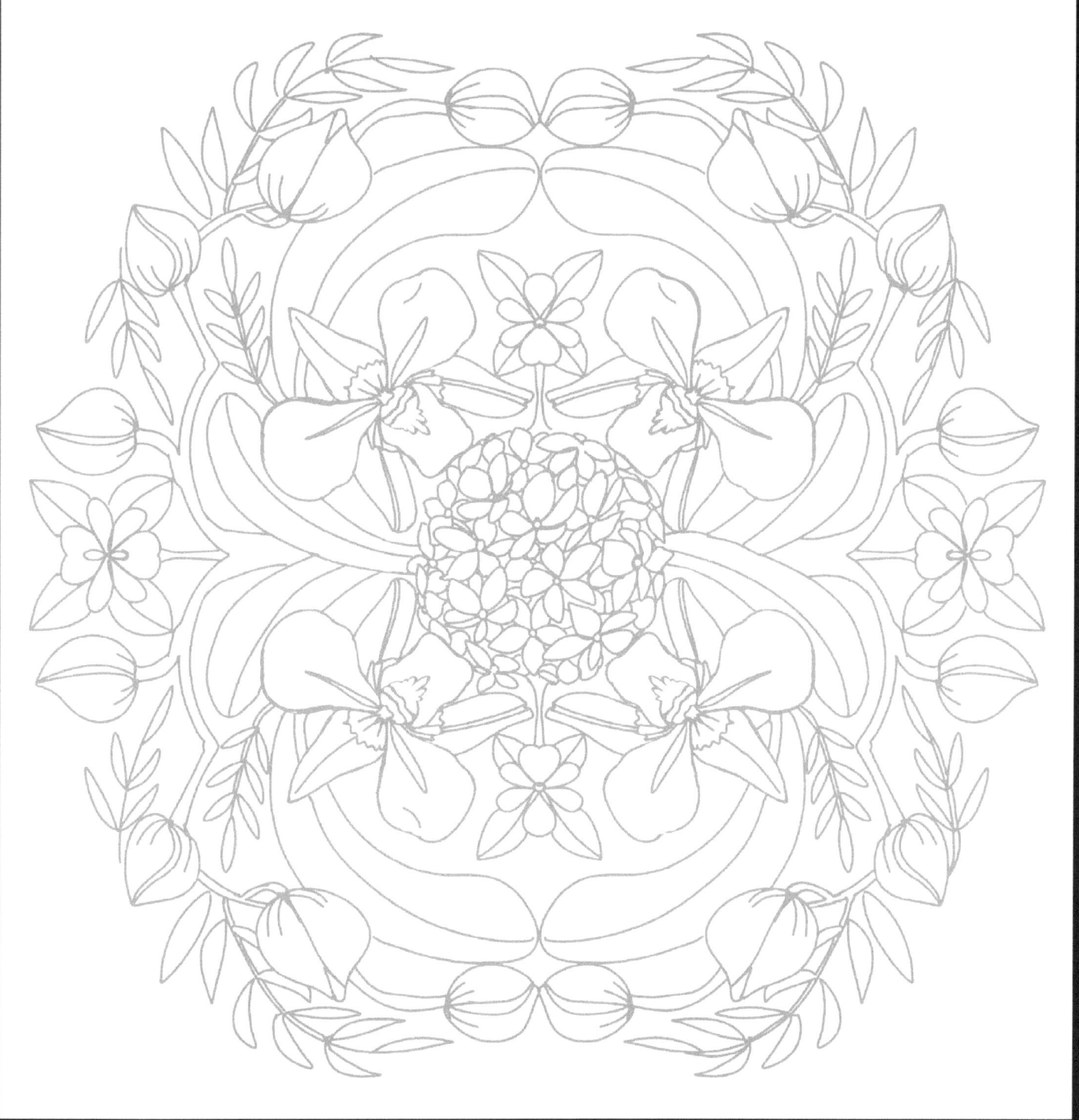

I am starting to see how wonderful life can be!

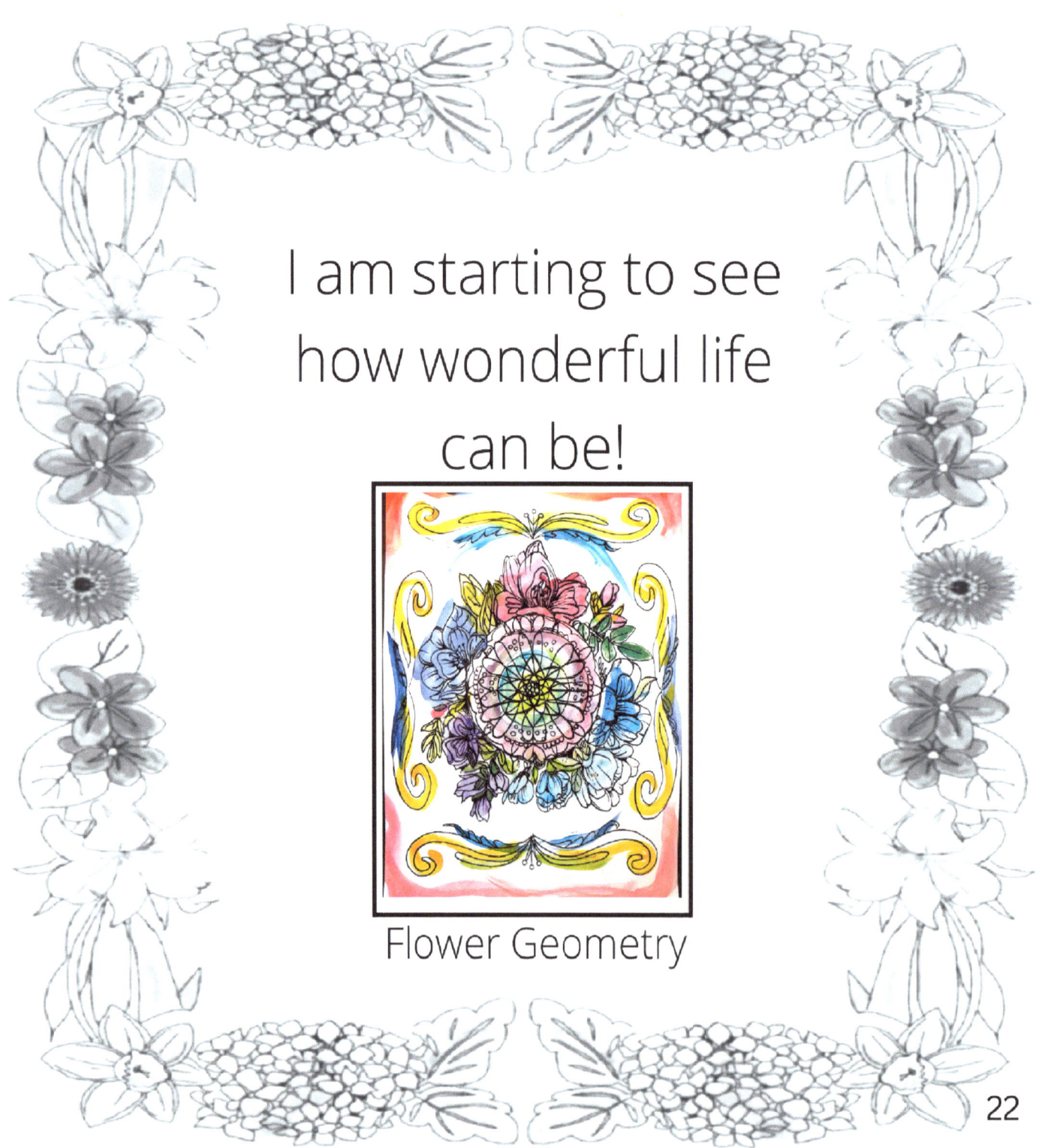

Flower Geometry

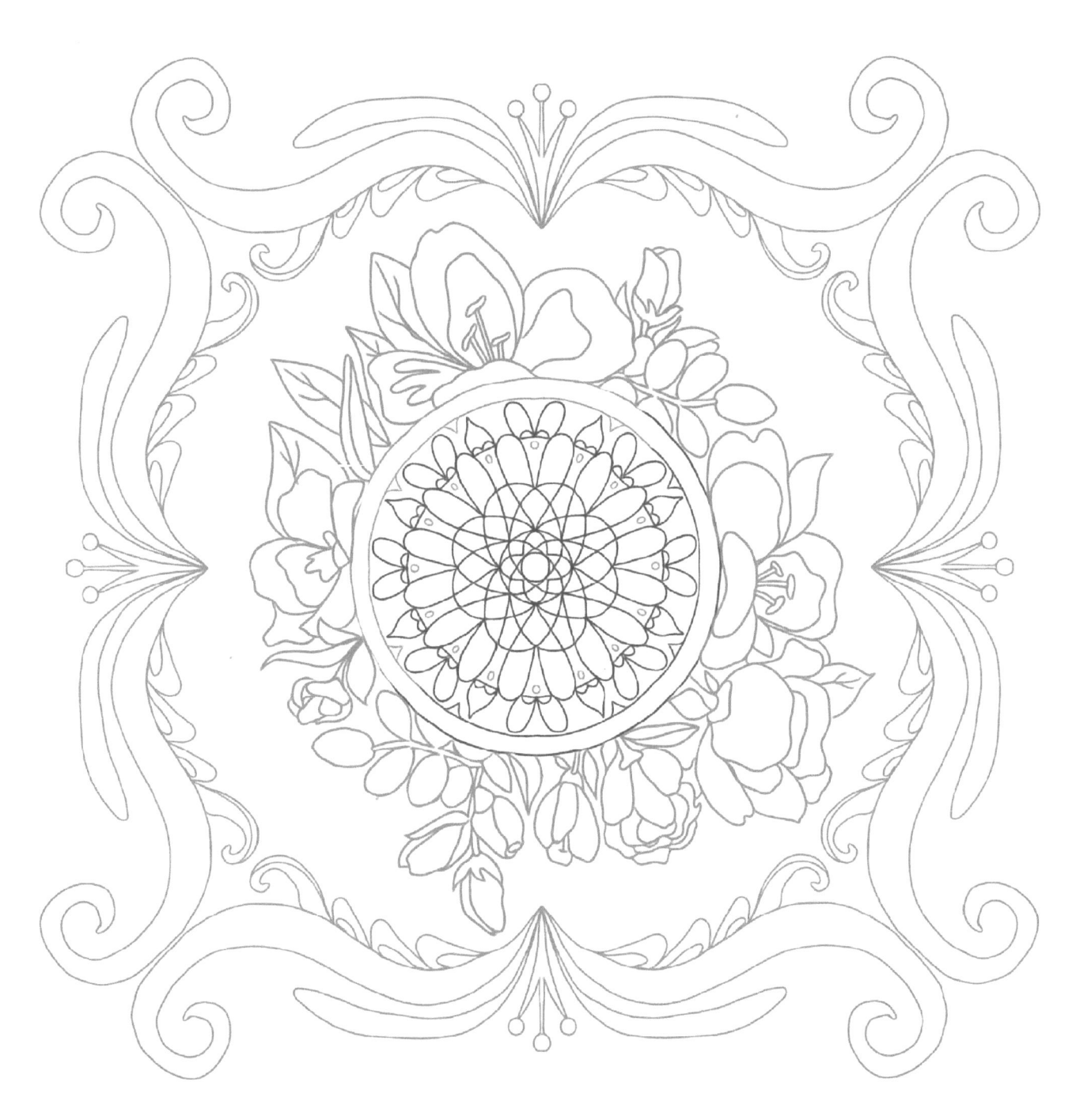

A technique to try

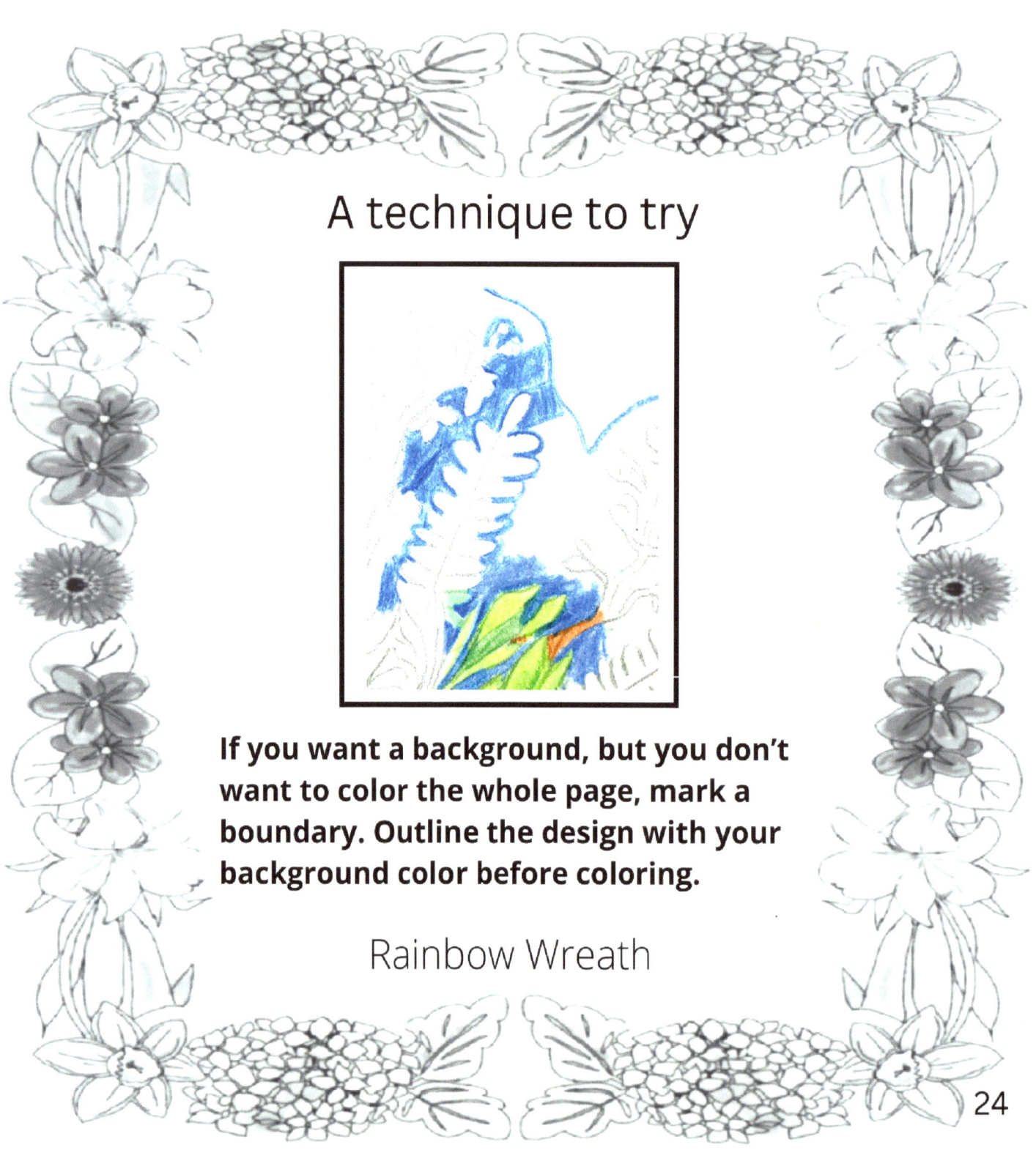

If you want a background, but you don't want to color the whole page, mark a boundary. Outline the design with your background color before coloring.

Rainbow Wreath

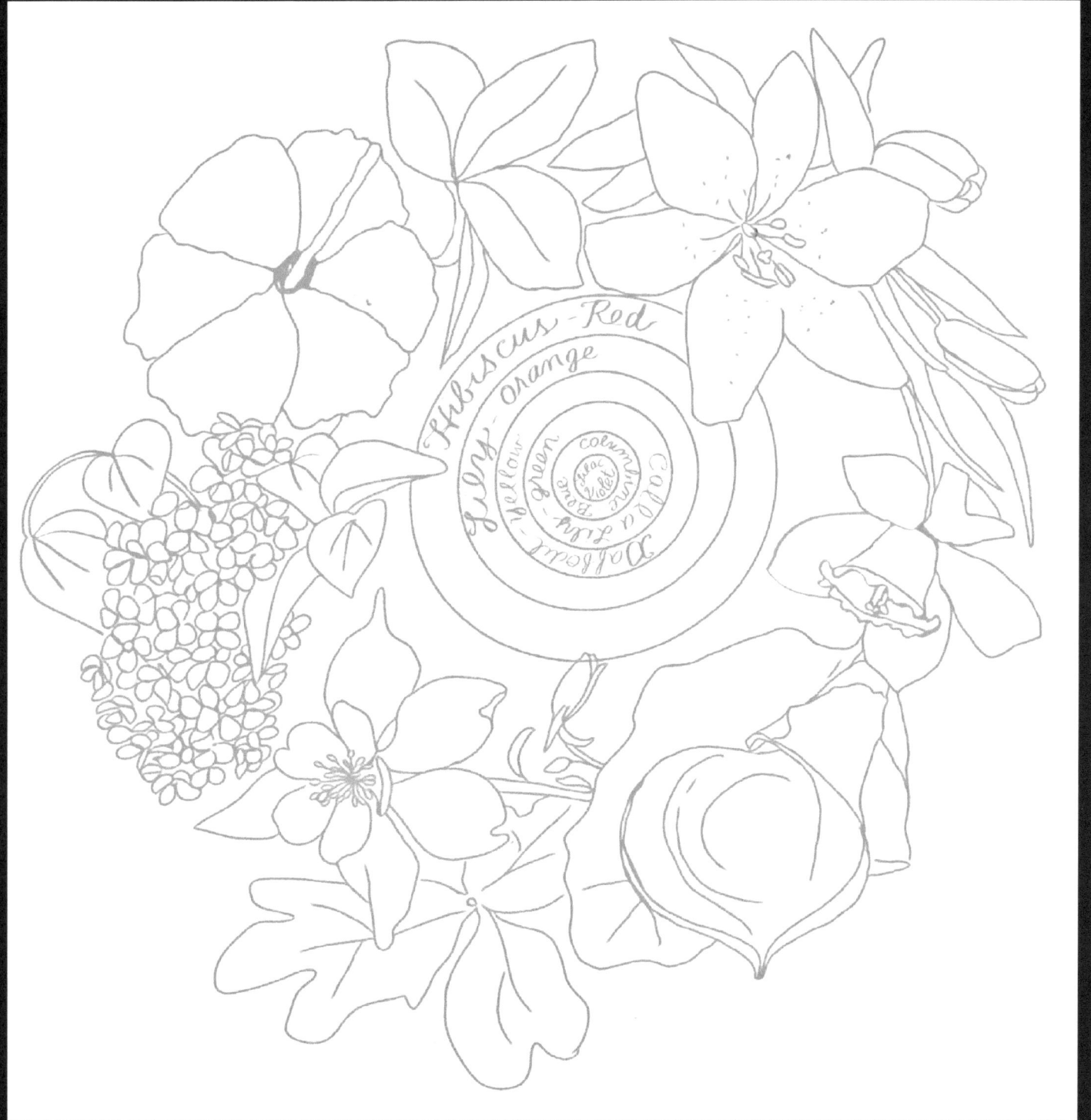

I am a pro at responding gently with my words and actions rather than reacting harshly.

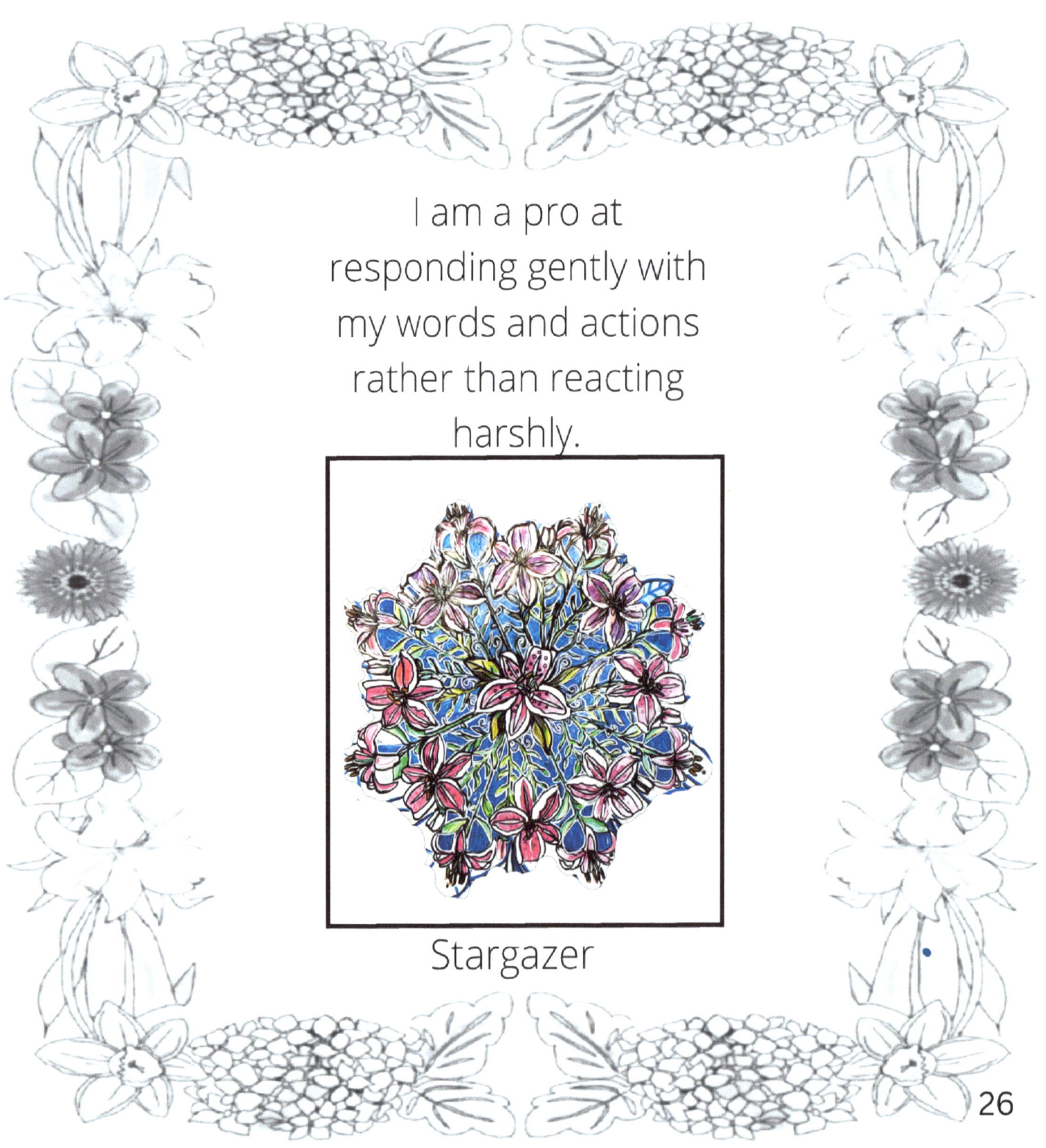

Stargazer

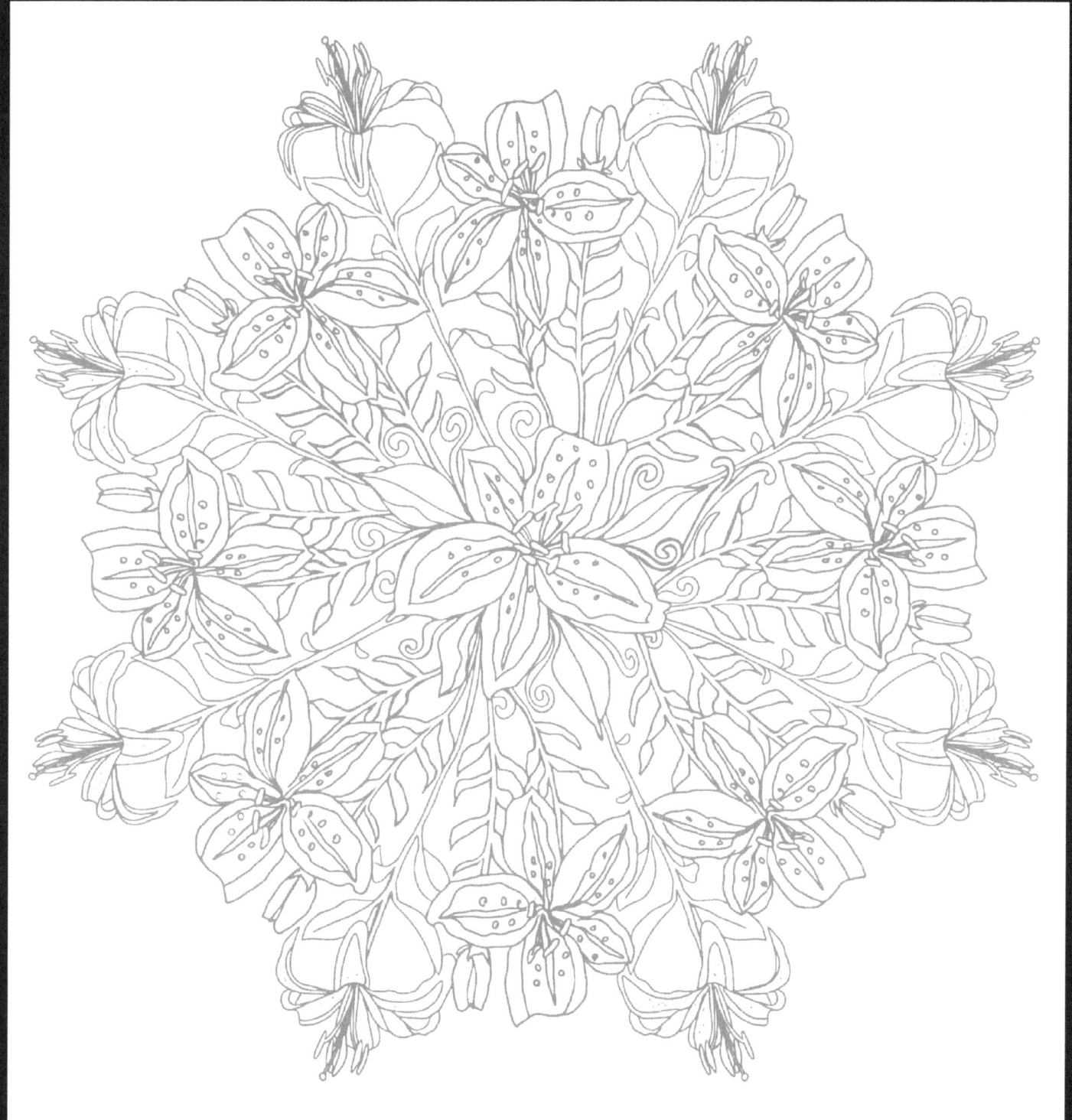

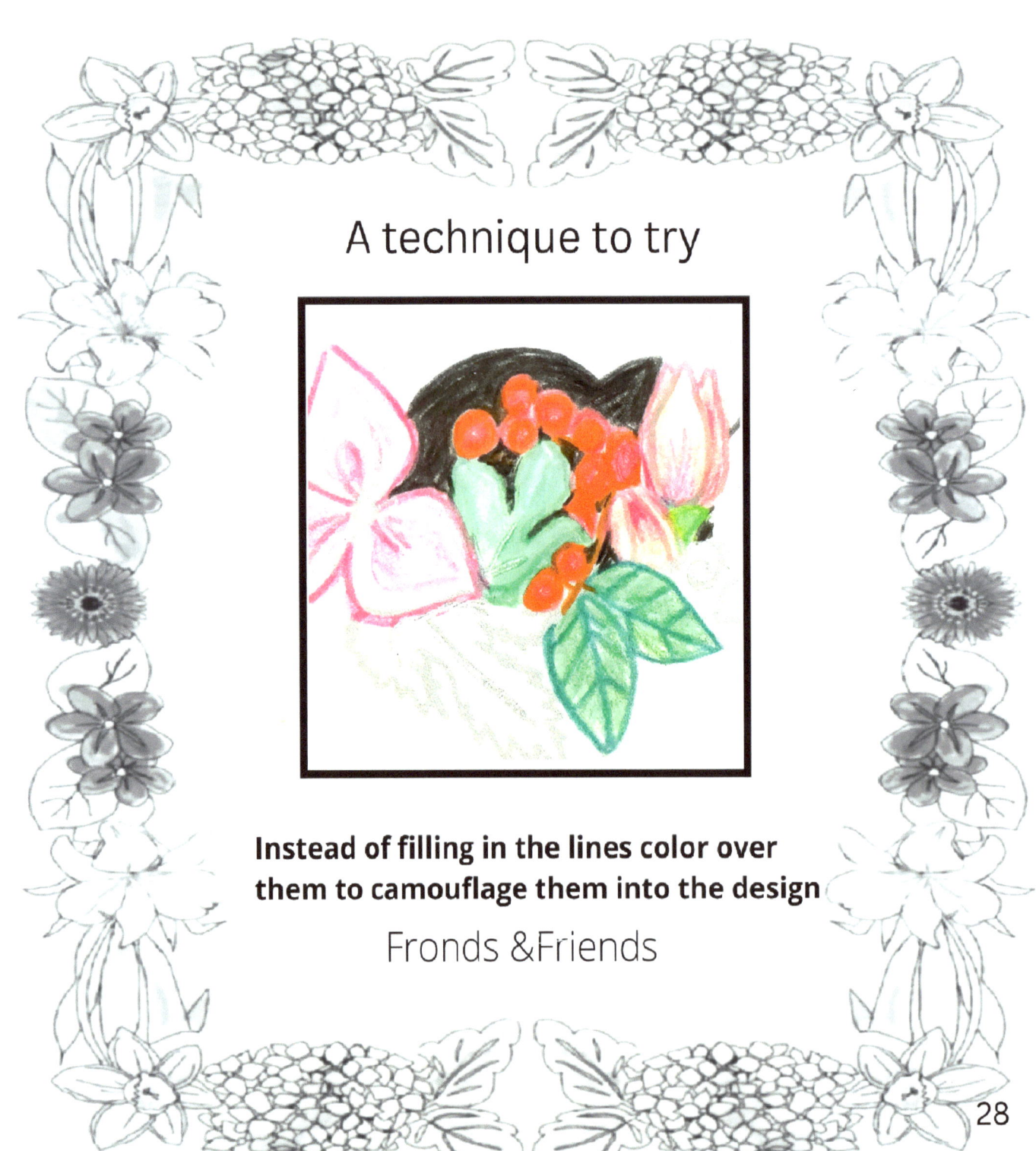

A technique to try

Instead of filling in the lines color over them to camouflage them into the design

Fronds &Friends

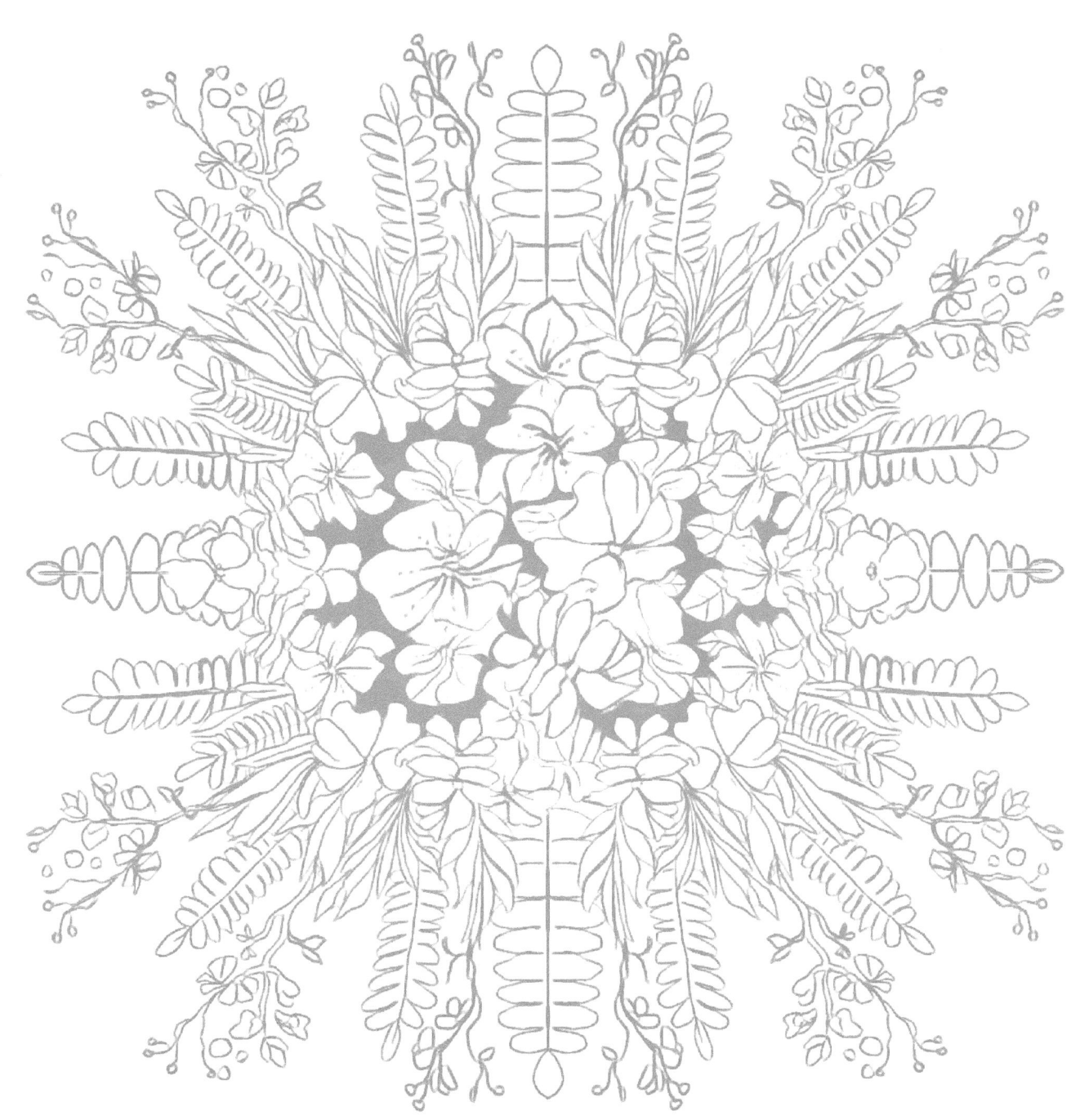

Craft Ideas

* Cut out your pages or make photocopies and frame or decoupage on wood for wall art
* Slide a copy into a tumbler sleeve for an enviable cup
* Cover a box, journal, candle, vase, or bottle
* Make a greeting card, gift tag, or gift wrap
* Collage it into another art piece
* Trace your clear phone case, cut out and insert into case.
* Glue to an old magnet or commercial sticker

Join the Community

Visit Terri Clauss Art on TikTok for demonstrations of the techniques mentioned here and others. Follow Lightgirl Design on Facebook and Instagram and join Terri's VIP Facebook group where our creative friends share our achievements. Post your picture on Instagram #lightgirldesign, and see what others have done. Terri can't wait to see what you do and read your stories.

www.ingramcontent.com/pod-product-compliance
Lightning Source LLC
Chambersburg PA
CBHW041936240526
45473CB00034B/1736